By George Santayana

THE REALM OF ESSENCE
THE REALM OF MATTER
PLATONISM AND THE SPIRITUAL LIFE
DIALOGUES IN LIMBO
POEMS
SCEPTICISM AND ANIMAL FAITH
SOLILOQUIES IN ENGLAND AND LATER
    SOLILOQUIES
CHARACTER   AND   OPINION   IN   THE
    UNITED STATES
THE SENSE OF BEAUTY
INTERPRETATIONS OF POETRY AND RE-
    LIGION
THE HERMIT OF CARMEL AND OTHER
    POEMS
WINDS OF DOCTRINE

THE LIFE OF REASON: OR THE PHASES OF
    HUMAN PROGRESS

I. Introduction and Reason in
        Common Sense
II. Reason in Society
III. Reason in Religion
IV. Reason in Art
V. Reason in Science

Little Essays Drawn from the Works
of George Santayana. By LOGAN
PEARSALL SMITH, *with the collabora-
tion of the Author.*

Charles Scribner's Sons

POEMS

POEMS

By GEORGE SANTAYANA

SELECTED BY THE AUTHOR
AND REVISED

NEW YORK
CHARLES SCRIBNER'S SONS
1935

CONTENTS

v

PREFACE

NEW editions of books are a venture for publishers rather than authors. The author has committed his rash act once for all at the beginning and he can hardly retract or repeat it. Nevertheless if I had not connived and collaborated at this selection of verses written (almost all of them) in my younger days, they probably would not have reappeared. I therefore owe an apology to my best critics and friends, who have always warned me that I am no poet; all the more since, in the sense in which they mean the word, I heartily agree with them. Of impassioned tenderness or Dionysiac frenzy I have nothing, nor even of that magic and pregnancy of phrase—really the creation of a fresh idiom—which marks the high lights of poetry. Even if my temperament had been naturally warmer, the fact that the English language (and I can write no other with assurance) was not my mother-tongue would of itself preclude any inspired use of it on my part; its roots do not quite reach to my centre. I never drank in in childhood the homely cadences and ditties which in pure spontaneous poetry set the essential key. I know no words redolent of the wonder-world, the fairy-tale, or the cradle. Moreover, I am city-bred, and that companionship with nature, those rural notes, which for English poets are almost inseparable from poetic feeling, fail me altogether. Landscape to me is only a background for fable or a symbol for fate, as it was to the ancients; and the human scene itself is but a theme for reflection. Nor have I been tempted into the by-ways even of towns, or fascinated by the aspect and humours of all sorts and conditions of men. My approach to language is literary, my images are only metaphors, and sometimes it seems to me that I resemble my countryman Don Quixote, when in his airy flights he was merely perched on a high horse and a wooden Pegasus; and I ask myself if I ever had anything to say in verse that might not have been said better in prose.

And yet, in reality, there was no such alternative. What I felt when I composed those verses could not have been rendered in

any other form. Their sincerity is absolute,
not only in respect to the thought which might
be abstracted from them and expressed in
prose, but also in respect to the aura of literary
and religious associations which envelops them.
If their prosody is worn and traditional, like a
liturgy, it is because they represent the initia-
tion of a mind into a world older and larger
than itself; not the chance experiences of a
stray individual, but his submission to what
is not his chance experience; to the truth of
nature and the moral heritage of mankind.
Here is the uncertain hand of an apprentice,
but of an apprentice in a great school. Verse
is one of the traditions of literature. Like the
orders of Greek architecture, the sonnet or the
couplet or the quatrain are better than anything
else that has been devised to serve the same
function; and the innate freedom of poets to
hazard new forms does not abolish the freedom
of all men to adopt the old ones. It is almost
inevitable that a man of letters, if his mind is
cultivated and capable of moral concentration,
should versify occasionally, or should have
versified. He need not on that account pose
as a poetic genius, and yet his verses (like those
of Michael Angelo, for instance) may form a

part, even if a subordinate part, of the expression
of his mind. Poetry was made for man, not
man for poetry, and there are really as many
kinds of it as there are poets, or even verses.
Is Hamlet's Soliloquy poetry? Would it have
conveyed its meaning better if not reined in
by the metre, and made to prance and turn to
the cadences of blank verse? Whether better
or worse, it would certainly not be itself without
that movement. Versification is like a pulsing
accompaniment, somehow sustaining and exalt-
ing the clear logic of the words. The accompaniment may be orchestral, but it is not
necessarily worse for being thrummed on a
mandolin or a guitar. So the couplets of Pope
or Dryden need not be called poetry, but they
could not have been prose. They frame in a
picture, balanced like the dance. There is an
elevation, too, in poetic diction, just because
it is consecrated and archaic; a pomp as of
a religious procession, without which certain
intuitions would lose all their grace and dignity.
Borrowed plumes would not even seem an
ornament if they were not in themselves
beautiful. To say that what was good once
is good no longer is to give too much im-
portance to chronology. Æsthetic fashions may

that this world, with himself in it, should be
the strange world which it is. Everything he
thinks or utters will accordingly be an integral
part of his philosophy, whether it be called
poetry or science or criticism. The verses of a
philosopher will be essentially epigrams, like
those which the Greek sages composed; they
will moralise the spectacle, whether it be some
personal passion or some larger aspect of
nature.

My own moral philosophy, especially as
expressed in this more sentimental form, may
not seem very robust or joyous. Its fortitude
and happiness are those of but one type of soul.
The owl hooting from his wintry bough cannot
be chanticleer crowing in the barnyard, yet he
is sacred to Minerva; and the universal poet,
who can sing the humours of winter no less
lustily than those of spring, may even speak
of his "merry note," worthy to mingle with
the other pleasant accidents of the somberer
season,

> When icicles hang by the wall,
> .   .   .   .   .   .
> And coughing drowns the parson's saw.

But whether the note seem merry or sad,
musical or uncouth, it is itself a note of nature;

and it may at least be commended, seeing it
conveys a philosophy, for not conveying it by
argument, but frankly making confession of an
actual spiritual experience, addressed only to
those whose ear it may strike sympathetically
and who, crossing the same dark wood on their
own errands, may pause for a moment to listen
gladly.

G. S.

November 1922.

SONNETS

1883–1893

I

I sought on earth a garden of delight,
Or island altar to the Sea and Air,
Where gentle music were accounted prayer,
And reason, veiled, performed the happy rite.
My sad youth worshipped at the piteous height
Where God vouchsafed the death of man to share;
His love made mortal sorrow light to bear,
But his deep wounds put joy to shamèd flight.
And though his arms, outstretched upon the tree,
Were beautiful, and pleaded my embrace,
My sins were loth to look upon his face.
So came I down from Golgotha to thee,
Eternal Mother; let the sun and sea
Heal me, and keep me in thy dwelling-place.

X.

SLOW and reluctant was the long descent,
With many farewell pious looks behind,
And dumb misgivings where the path might wind,
And questionings of nature, as I went.
The greener branches that above me bent,
The broadening valleys, quieted my mind,
To the fair reasons of the Spring inclined
And to the Summer's tender argument.
But sometimes, as revolving night descended,
And in my childish heart the new song ended,
I lay down, full of longing, on the steep;
And, haunting still the lonely way I wended,
Into my dreams the ancient sorrow blended,
And with these holy echoes charmed my sleep.

III

O WORLD, thou choosest not the better part!
It is not wisdom to be only wise,
And on the inward vision close the eyes,
But it is wisdom to believe the heart.
Columbus found a world, and had no chart,
Save one that faith deciphered in the skies;
To trust the soul's invincible surmise
Was all his science and his only art.
Our knowledge is a torch of smoky pine
That lights the pathway but one step ahead
Across a void of mystery and dread.
Bid, then, the tender light of faith to shine
By which alone the mortal heart is led
Unto the thinking of the thought divine.

IV

I WOULD I had been born in nature's day,
When man was in the world a wide-eyed boy,
And clouds of sorrow crossed his sky of joy
To scatter dewdrops on the buds of May.
Then could he work and love and fight and pray,
Nor heartsick grow in fortune's long employ.
Mighty to build and ruthless to destroy
He lived, while maskèd death unquestioned lay.
Now ponder we the ruins of the years,
And groan beneath the weight of boasted gain;
No unsung bacchanal can charm our ears
And lead our dances to the woodland fane,
No hope of heaven sweeten our few tears
And hush the importunity of pain.

V

Dreamt I to-day the dream of yesternight,
Sleep ever feigning one evolving theme,—
Of my two lives which should I call the dream?
Which action vanity? which vision sight?
Some greater waking must pronounce aright,
If aught abideth of the things that seem,
And with both currents swell the flooded stream
Into an ocean infinite of light.
Even such a dream I dream, and know full well
My waking passeth like a midnight spell,
But know not if my dreaming breaketh through
Into the deeps of heaven and of hell.
I know but this of all I would I knew:
Truth is a dream, unless my dream is true.

VI

Love not as do the flesh-imprisoned men
Whose dreams are of a bitter bought caress,
Or even of a maiden's tenderness
Whom they love only that she loves again.
For it is but thyself thou lovest then,
Or what thy thoughts would glory to possess;
But love thou nothing thou wouldst love the less
If henceforth ever hidden from thy ken.
Love but the formless and eternal Whole
From whose effulgence one unheeded ray
Breaks on this prism of dissolving clay
Into the flickering colours of thy soul.
These flash and vanish; bid them not to stay,
For wisdom brightens as they fade away.

VII

I WOULD I might forget that I am I,
And break the heavy chain that binds me fast,
Whose links about myself my deeds have cast.
What in the body's tomb doth buried lie
Is boundless; 'tis the spirit of the sky,
Lord of the future, guardian of the past,
And soon must forth, to know his own at last.
In his large life to live, I fain would die.
Happy the dumb beast, hungering for food,
But calling not his suffering his own;
Blessèd the angel, gazing on all good,
But knowing not he sits upon a throne;
Wretched the mortal, pondering his mood,
And doomed to know his aching heart alone.

VIII

O MARTYRED Spirit of this helpless Whole,
Who dost by pain for tyranny atone,
And in the star, the atom, and the stone,
Purgest the primal guilt, and in the soul;
Rich but in grief, thou dost thy wealth unroll,
And givest of thy substance to thine own,
Mingling the love, the laughter, and the groan
In the large hollow of the heaven's bowl.
Fill full my cup; the dregs and honeyed brim
I take from thy just hand, more worthy love
For sweetening not the draught for me or him.
What in myself I am, that let me prove;
Relent not for my feeble prayer, nor dim
The burning of thine altar for my hymn.

IX

Have patience; it is fit that in this wise
The spirit purge away its proper dross.
No endless fever doth thy watches toss,
For by excess of evil, evil dies.
Soon shall the faint world melt before thine eyes,
And, all life's losses cancelled by life's loss,
Thou shalt lay down all burdens on thy cross,
And be that day with God in Paradise.
Have patience; for a long eternity
No summons woke thee from thy happy sleep;
For love of God one vigil thou canst keep
And add thy drop of sorrow to the sea.
Having known grief, all will be well with thee,
Ay, and thy second slumber will be deep.

X

HAVE I the heart to wander on the earth,
So patient in her everlasting course,
Seeking no prize, but bowing to the force
That gives direction and hath given birth?
Rain tears, sweet Pity, to refresh my dearth,
And plough my sterile bosom, sharp Remorse,
That I grow sick and curse my being's source
If haply one day passes lacking mirth.
Doth the sun therefore burn, that I may bask?
Or do the tirèd earth and tireless sea,
That toil not for their pleasure, toil for me?
Amid the world's long striving, wherefore ask
What reasons were, or what rewards shall be?
The covenant God gave us is a task.

XI

Deem not, because you see me in the press
Of this world's children run my fated race,
That I blaspheme against a proffered grace,
Or leave unlearned the love of holiness.
I honour not that sanctity the less
Whose aureole illumines not my face,
But dare not tread the secret, holy place
To which the priest and prophet have access.
For some are born to be beatified
By anguish, and by grievous penance done;
And some, to furnish forth the age's pride,
And to be praised of men beneath the sun;
And some are born to stand perplexed aside
From so much sorrow—of whom I am one.

XII

Mightier storms than this are brewed on earth
That pricks the crystal lake with summer showers.
The past hath treasure of sublimer hours,
And God is witness to their changeless worth.
Big is the future with portentous birth
Of battles numberless, and nature's powers
Outdo my dreams of beauty in the flowers,
And top my revels with the demons' mirth.
But thou, glad river that hast reached the plain,
Scarce wak'st the rushes to a slumberous sigh.
The mountains sleep behind thee, and the main
Awaits thee, lulling an eternal pain
With patience; nor doth Phœbe, throned on high,
The mirror of thy placid heart disdain.

XIII

SWEET are the days we wander with no hope
Along life's labyrinthine trodden way,
With no impatience at the steep's delay,
Nor sorrow at the swift-descended slope.
Why this inane curiosity to grope
In the dim dust for gems' unmeaning ray?
Why this proud piety, that dares to pray
For a world wider than the heaven's cope?
Farewell, my burden! No more will I bear
The foolish load of my fond faith's despair,
But trip the idle race with careless feet.
The crown of olive let another wear;
It is my crown to mock the runner's heat
With gentle wonder and with laughter sweet.

XIV

THERE may be chaos still around the world,
This little world that in my thinking lies;
For mine own bosom is the paradise
Where all my life's fair visions are unfurled.
Within my nature's shell I slumber curled,
Unmindful of the changing outer skies,
Where now, perchance, some new-born Eros flies,
Or some old Cronos from his throne is hurled.
I heed them not; or if the subtle night
Haunt me with deities I never saw,
I soon mine eyelid's drowsy curtain draw
To hide their myriad faces from my sight.
They threat in vain; the whirlwind cannot awe
A happy snow-flake dancing in the flaw.

XV

A WALL, a wall to hem the azure sphere,
And hedge me in from the disconsolate hills!
Give me but one of all the mountain rills,
Enough of ocean in its voice I hear.
Come no profane insatiate mortal near
With the contagion of his passionate ills;
The smoke of battle all the valleys fills,
Let the eternal sunlight greet me here.
This spot is sacred to the deeper soul
And to the piety that mocks no more.
In nature's inmost heart is no uproar,
None in this shrine; in peace the heavens roll,
In peace the slow tides pulse from shore to shore,
And ancient quiet broods from pole to pole.

XVI

A THOUSAND beauties that have never been
Haunt me with hope and tempt me to pursue;
The gods, methinks, dwell just behind the blue;
The satyrs at my coming fled the green.
The flitting shadows of the grove between
The dryads' eyes were winking, and I knew
The wings of sacred Eros as he flew
And left me to the love of things not seen.
'Tis a sad love, like an eternal prayer,
And knows no keen delight, no faint surcease.
Yet from the seasons hath the earth increase,
And heaven shines as if the gods were there.
Had Dian passed there could no deeper peace
Embalm the purple stretches of the air.

XVII

THERE was a time when in the teeth of fate
I flung the challenge of the spirit's right;
The child, the dreamer of that visioned night,
Woke, and was humbled unto man's estate.
A slave I am; on sun and moon I wait,
Who heed not that I live upon their light.
Me they despise, but are themselves so bright
They flood my heart with love, and quench my hate.
O subtle Beauty, sweet persuasive worth
That didst the love of being first inspire,
We do thee homage both in death and birth.
Thirsting for thee, we die in thy great dearth,
Or borrow breath of infinite desire
To chase thine image through the haunted earth.

XVIII

Blaspheme not love, ye lovers, nor dispraise
The wise divinity that makes you blind,
Sealing the eyes, but showing to the mind
The high perfection from which nature strays.
For love is God, and in unfathomed ways
Brings forth the beauty for which fancy pined.
I loved, and lost my love among mankind;
But I have found it after many days.
Oh, trust in God, and banish rash despair,
That, feigning evil, is itself the curse!
My angel is come back, more sad and fair,
And witness to the truth of love I bear,
With too much rapture for this sacred verse,
At the exceeding answer to my prayer.

XIX

Above the battlements of heaven rise
The glittering domes of the gods' golden dwelling,
Whence, like a constellation, passion-quelling,
The truth of all things feeds immortal eyes.
There all forgotten dreams of paradise
From the deep caves of memory upwelling,
All tender joys beyond our dim foretelling
Are ever bright beneath the flooded skies.
There we live o'er, amid angelic powers,
Our lives without remorse, as if not ours,
And others' lives with love, as if our own;
For we behold, from those eternal towers,
The deathless beauty of all wingèd hours,
And have our being in their truth alone.

XX

THESE strewn thoughts, by the mountain pathway
    sprung,
I conned for comfort, till I ceased to grieve,
And with these flowering thorns I dare to weave
The crown, great Mother, on thine altar hung.
Teach thou a larger speech to my loosed tongue,
And to mine opened eyes thy secrets give,
That in thy perfect love I learn to live,
And in thine immortality be young.
The soul is not on earth an alien thing
That hath her life's rich sources otherwhere;
She is a parcel of the sacred air.
She takes her being from the breath of Spring,
The glance of Phœbus is her fount of light,
And her long sleep a draught of primal night.

SONNETS

1895

XXI

AMONG the myriad voices of the Spring
What were the voice of my supreme desire,
What were my cry amid the vernal choir,
Or my complaint before the gods that sing?
O too late love, O flight on wounded wing,
Infinite hope my lips should not suspire,
Why, when the world is thine, my grief require,
Or mock my dear-bought patience with thy sting?
Though I be mute, the birds will in the boughs
Sing as in every April they have sung,
And, though I die, the incense of heart-vows
Will float to heaven, as when I was young.
But, O ye beauties I must never see,
How great a lover have you lost in me!

XXII

'Tis love that moveth the celestial spheres
In endless yearning for the Changeless One,
And the stars sing together, as they run
To number the innumerable years.
'Tis love that lifteth through their dewy tears
The roses' beauty to the heedless sun,
And with no hope, nor any guerdon won,
Love leads me on, nor end of love appears.
For the same breath that did awake the flowers,
Making them happy with a joy unknown,
Kindled my light and fixed my spirit's goal;
And the same hand that reined the flying hours
And chained the whirling earth to Phœbus' throne,
In love's eternal orbit keeps the soul.

XXIII

But is this love, that in my hollow breast
Gnaws like a silent poison, till I faint?
Is this the vision that the haggard saint
Fed with his vigils, till he found his rest?
Is this the hope that piloted thy quest,
Knight of the Grail, and kept thy heart from taint?
Is this the heaven, poets, that ye paint?
Oh, then, how like damnation to be blest!
This is not love: it is that worser thing—
Hunger for love, while love is yet to learn.
Thy peace is gone, my soul; thou long must yearn.
Long is thy winter's pilgrimage, till spring
And late home-coming; long ere thou return
To where the seraphs covet not, and burn.

XXIV

ALTHOUGH I decked a chamber for my bride,
And found a moonlit garden for the tryst
Wherein all flowers looked happy as we kissed,
Hath the deep heart of me been satisfied?
The chasm 'twixt our spirits yawns as wide
Though our lips meet, and clasp thee as I list,
The something perfect that I love is missed,
And my warm worship freezes into pride.
But why—O waywardness of nature!—why
Seek farther in the world? I had my choice,
And we said we were happy, you and I.
Why in the forest should I hear a cry,
Or in the sea an unavailing voice,
Or feel a pang to look upon the sky?

XXV

As in the midst of battle there is room
For thoughts of love, and in foul sin for mirth;
As gossips whisper of a trinket's worth
Spied by the death-bed's flickering candle-gloom;
As in the crevices of Cæsar's tomb
The sweet herbs flourish on a little earth:
So in this great disaster of our birth
We can be happy, and forget our doom.
For morning, with a ray of tenderest joy
Gilding the iron heaven, hides the truth,
And evening gently woos us to employ
Our grief in idle catches.   Such is youth;
Till from that summer's trance we wake, to find
Despair before us, vanity behind.

XXVI

Oh, if the heavy last unuttered groan
That lieth here could issue to the air,
Then might God's peace descend on my despair
And seal this heart as with a mighty stone.
For what sin, Heaven, must I thus atone?
Was it a sin to love what seemed so fair?
If thou deny me hope, why give me care?
I have not lived, and die alone, alone.
This is not new.   Many have perished so.
Long years of nothing, with some days of grief,
Made their sad life.   Their own hand sought relief
Too late to find it, impotently slow.
I know, strong Fate, the trodden way I go.
Joy lies behind me.   Be the journey brief.

XXVII

Sleep hath composed the anguish of my brain,
And ere the dawn I will arise and pray.
Strengthen me, Heaven, and attune my lay
Unto my better angel's clear refrain.
For I can hear him in the night again,
The breathless night, snow-smothered, happy, grey,
With premonition of the jocund day,
Singing a quiet carol to my pain.
Slowly, saith he, the April buds are growing
In the chill core of twigs all leafless now;
Gently, beneath the weight of last night's snowing,
Patient of winter's hand, the branches bow.
Each buried seed lacks light as much as thou.
Wait for the spring, brave heart; there is no knowing.

XXVIII

Out of the dust the queen of roses springs;
The brackish depths of the blown waters bear
Blossoms of foam; the common mist and air
Weave Vesper's holy, pity-laden wings.
So from sad, mortal, and unhallowed things
Bud stars that in their crowns the angels wear;
And worship of the infinitely fair
Flows from thine eyes, as wise Petrarca sings:
"Hence comes the understanding of love's scope,
That, seeking thee, to perfect good aspires,
Accounting little what all flesh desires;
And hence the spirit's happy pinions ope
In flight impetuous to the heaven's choirs:
Wherefore I walk already proud in hope."

XXIX

WHAT riches have you that you deem me poor,
Or what large comfort that you call me sad?
Tell me what makes you so exceeding glad:
Is your earth happy or your heaven sure?
I hope for heaven, since the stars endure
And bring such tidings as our fathers had.
I know no deeper doubt to make me mad,
I need no brighter love to keep me pure.
To me the faiths of old are daily bread;
I bless their hope, I bless their will to save,
And my deep heart still meaneth what they said.
It makes me happy that the soul is brave,
And, being so much kinsman to the dead,
I walk contented to the peopled grave.

XXX

Let my lips touch thy lips, and my desire
Contagious fever be, to set a-glow
The blood beneath thy whiter breast than snow—
Wonderful snow, that so can kindle fire!
Abandon to what gods in us conspire
Thy little wisdom, sweetest; for they know.
Is it not something that I love thee so?
Take that from life, ere death thine all require.
But no! Then would a mortal warmth disperse
That beauteous snow to water-drops, which, turned
To marble, had escaped the primal curse.
Be still a goddess, till my heart have burned
Its sacrifice before thee, and my verse
Told this late world the love that I have learned.

XXXI

A BROTHER's love, but that I chose thee out
From all the world, not by the chance of birth,
But in the risen splendour of thy worth,
Which, like the sun, put all my stars to rout.
A lover's love, but that it bred no doubt
Of love returned, no heats of flood and dearth,
But, asking nothing, found in all the earth
The consolation of a heart devout.
A votary's love, though with no pale and wild
Imaginations did I stretch the might
Of a sweet friendship and a mortal light.
Thus in my love all loves are reconciled
That purest be, and in my prayer the right
Of brother, lover, friend, and eremite.

XXXII

Let not thy bosom, to my foes allied,
Insult my sorrow with this coat of mail,
When for thy strong defence, if love assail,
Thou hast the world, thy virtue, and my pride.
But if thine own dear eyes I see beside
Sharpened against me, then my strength will fail,
Abandoning sail and rudder to the gale
For thy sweet sake alone so long defied.
If I am poor, in death how rich and brave
Will seem my spirit with the love it gave;
If I am sad, I shall seem happy then.
Be mine, be mine in God and in the grave,
Since naught but chance and the insensate wave
Divides us, and the wagging tongue of men.

XXXIII

A PERFECT love is nourished by despair.
I am thy pupil in the school of pain;
Mine eyes will not reproach thee for disdain,
But thank thy rich disdain for being fair.
Aye! the proud sorrow, the eternal prayer
Thy beauty taught, what shall unteach again?
Hid from my sight, thou livest in my brain;
Fled from my bosom, thou abidest there.
And though they buried thee, and called thee dead,
And told me I should never see thee more,
The violets that grew above thy head
Would waft thy breath and tell thy sweetness o'er,
And every rose thy scattered ashes bred
Would to my sense thy loveliness restore.

XXXIV

THOUGH destiny half broke her cruel bars,
Herself contriving we should meet on earth,
And with thy beauty fed my spirit's dearth
And tuned to love the ages' many jars,
Yet there is potency in natal stars;
And we were far divided in our birth
By nature's gifts and half the planet's girth,
And speech, and faith, and blood, and ancient wars.
Alas! thy very radiance made division,
Thy youth, thy friends, and all men's eyes that wooed;
Thy simple kindness came as in derision
Of so much love and so much solitude;
Or did the good gods order all to show
How far the single strength of love can go?

XXXV

We needs must be divided in the tomb,
For I would die among the hills of Spain,
And o'er the treeless melancholy plain
Await the coming of the final gloom.
But thou—O pitiful!—wilt find scant room
Among thy kindred by the northern main,
And fade into the drifting mist again,
The hemlocks' shadow, or the pines' perfume.
Let gallants lie beside their ladies' dust,
In one cold grave, with mortal love inurned;
Let the sea part our ashes, if it must.
The souls fled thence which love immortal burned,
For they were wedded without bond of lust,
And nothing of our heart to earth returned.

XXXVI

WE were together, and I longed to tell
How drop by silent drop my bosom bled.
I took some verses full of you, and read,
Waiting for God to work some miracle.
They told how love had plunged in burning hell
One half my soul, while the other half had fled
Upon love's wings to heaven; and you said:
"I like the verses; they are written well."
If I had knelt confessing "It is you,
You are my torment and my rapture too,"
I should have seen you rise in flushed disdain:
"For shame to say so, be it false or true!"
And the sharp sword that ran me through and through,
On your white bosom too had left a stain.

XXXVII

AND I was silent.   Now you do not know,
But read these very words with vacant eyes,
And, as you turn the page, peruse the skies,
And I go by you as a cloud might go.
You are not cruel, though you dealt the blow,
And I am happy, though I miss the prize;
For, when God tells you, you will not despise
The love I bore you.   It is better so.
My soul is just, and thine without a stain.
Why should not life divide us, whose division
Is frail and passing, as its union vain?
All things 'neath other planets will grow plain
When, as we wander through the fields Elysian,
Eternal echoes haunt us of this pain.

XXXVIII

Oh, not for me, for thee, dear God, her head
Shines with this perfect golden aureole,
For thee this sweetness doth possess her soul,
And to thy chambers are her footsteps led.
The light will live that on my path she shed,
While any pilgrim yet hath any goal,
And heavenly musicians from their scroll
Will sing all her sweet words, when I am dead.
In her unspotted heart is steadfast faith
Fed on high thoughts, and in her beauteous face
The fountain of the love that conquers death;
And as I see her in her kneeling-place,
A Gabriel comes, and with inaudible breath
Whispers within me: Hail, thou full of grace.

XXXIX

The world will say, "What mystic love is this?
What ghostly mistress?   What angelic friend?"
Read, masters, your own passion to the end,
And tell me then if I have writ amiss.
When all loves die that hang upon a kiss,
And must with cavil and with chance contend,
Their risen selves with the eternal blend
Where perfect dying is their perfect bliss.
And might I kiss her once, asleep or dead,
Upon the forehead or the globèd eyes,
Or where the gold is parted on her head,
That kiss would help me on to paradise
As if I kissed the consecrated bread
In which the buried soul of Jesus lies.

XL

If, when the story of my love is old,
This book should live and lover's leisure feed,
Fair charactered, for bluest eye to read,—
And richly bound, for whitest hand to hold,—
O limn me then this lovely head in gold,
And, limner, the soft lips and lashes heed,
And set her in the midst, my love indeed,
The sweet eyes tender, and the broad brow cold.
And never let thy colours think to cast
A brighter splendour on her beauties past,
Or venture to disguise a fancied flaw;
Let not thy painting falsify my rhyme,
But perfect keep the mould for after time,
And let the whole world see her as I saw.

XLI

YET why, of one who loved thee not, command
Thy counterfeit, for other men to see,
When God himself did on my heart for me
Thy face, like Christ's upon the napkin, brand?
O how much subtler than a painter's hand
Is love to render back the truth of thee!
My soul should be thy glass in time to be,
And in my thought thine effigy should stand.
Yet, lest the churlish critics of that age
Should flout my praise, and deem a lover's rage
Could gild a virtue and a grace exceed,
I bid thine image here confront my page,
That men may look upon thee as they read,
And cry: Such eyes a better poet need.

XLII

As when the sceptre dangles from the hand
Of some king doting, faction runneth wild,
Thieves shake their chains and traitors, long exiled,
Hover about the confines of the land,
Till the young Prince, anointed, takes command,
Full of high purpose, simple, trustful, mild,
And, smitten by his radiance undefiled,
The ruffians are abashed, the cowards stand:—
So in my kingdom riot and despair
Lived by thy lack, and called for thy control,
But at thy coming all the world grew fair;
Away before thy face the villains stole,
And panoplied I rose to do and bear,
When love his clarion sounded in my soul.

XLIII

THE candour of the gods is in thy gaze,
The strength of Dian in thy virgin hand,
Commanding as the goddess might command,
And lead her lovers into higher ways.
Aye, the gods walk among us in these days,
Had we the docile soul to understand;
And me they visit in this joyless land,
To cheer mine exile and receive my praise.
For once, methinks, before the angels fell,
Thou, too, didst follow the celestial seven
Threading in file the meads of asphodel.
And when thou comest, lady, where I dwell,
The place is flooded with the light of heaven
And a lost music I remember well.

XLIV

For thee the sun doth daily rise, and set
Behind the curtain of the hills of sleep,
And my soul, passing through the nether deep
Broods on thy love, and never can forget.
For thee the garlands of the wood are wet,
For thee the daisies up the meadow's sweep
Stir in the sidelong light, and for thee weep
The drooping ferns above the violet.
For thee the labour of my studious ease
I ply with hope, for thee all pleasures please,
Thy sweetness doth the bread of sorrow leaven;
And from thy noble lips and heart of gold
I drink the comfort of the faiths of old,
And thy perfection is my proof of heaven.

XLV

Flower of the world, bright angel, single friend!
I never asked of Heaven thou shouldst love me;
As well ask Heaven's self that spreads above me
With all his stars about my head to bend
It is enough my spirit may ascend
And clasp the good whence nothing can remove me;
Enough, if faith and hope and love approve me,
And make me worthy of the blessed end.
And as a pilgrim from the path withdraws,
Seeing Christ carven on the holy rood,
And breathes an ave in the solitude,
So will I stop and pray—for I have cause—
And in all crossways of my thinking pause
Before thine image, saying: God is good.

XLVI

When I survey the harvest of the year
And from time's threshing garner up the grain,
What profit have I of forgotten pain,
What comfort, heart-locked, for the winter's cheer?
The season's yield is this, that thou art dear,
And that I love thee, that is all my gain;
The rest was chaff, blown from the weary brain
Where now thy treasured image lieth clear.
How liberal is beauty that, but seen,
Makes rich the bosom of her silent lover!
How excellent is truth, on which I lean!
Yet my religion were a charmed despair,
Did I not in thy perfect heart discover
How beauty can be true and virtue fair.

XLVII

Thou hast no name, or, if a name thou bearest,
To none it meaneth what it means to me:
Thy form, the loveliness the world can see,
Makes not the glory that to me thou wearest.
Nor thine unuttered thoughts, though they be fairest
And shaming all that in rude bosoms be:
All they are but the thousandth part of thee,
Which thou with blessed spirits haply sharest.
But incommunicable, peerless, dim,
Flooding my heart with anguish of despair,
Thou walkest, love, before me, shade of Him
Who only liveth, giveth, and is fair.
And constant ever, though inconstant known,
In all my loves I worshipped thee alone.

XLVIII

Of Helen's brothers, one was born to die
And one immortal, who, the fable saith,
Gave to the other that was nigh to death
One half his widowed immortality.
They would have lived and died alternately,
Breathing each other's warm transmuted breath,
Had not high Zeus, who justly ordereth,
Made them twin stars to shine eternally.
My heart was dying when thy flame of youth
Flooded its chambers through my gazing eyes.
My life is now thy beauty and thy truth.
Thou wouldst come down, forsaking paradise
To be my comfort, but by Heaven's ruth
I go to burn beside thee in the skies.

XLIX

AFTER grey vigils, sunshine in the heart;
After long fasting on the journey, food;
After sharp thirst, a draught of perfect good
To flood the soul, and heal her ancient smart.
Joy of my sorrow, never can we part;
Thou broodest o'er me in the haunted wood,
And with new music fill'st the solitude
By but so sweetly being what thou art.
He who hath made thee perfect, makes me blest.
O fiery minister, on mighty wings
Bear me, great love, to mine eternal rest.
Heaven it is to be at peace with things;
Come chaos now, and in a whirlwind's rings
Engulf the planets. I have seen the best.

L

Though utter death should swallow up my hope
And choke with dust the mouth of my desire,
Though no dawn burst, and no aurorean choir
Sing GLORIA DEO when the heavens ope,
Yet have I light of love, nor need to grope
Lost, wholly lost, without an inward fire;
The flame that quickeneth the world entire
Leaps in my breast, with cruel death to cope.
Hath not the night-environed earth her flowers?
Hath not my grief the blessed joy of thee?
Is not the comfort of these singing hours,
Full of thy perfectness, enough for me?
They are not evil, then, those hidden powers:
One love sufficeth an eternity.

MISCELLANEOUS SONNETS

ON A VOLUME OF SCHOLASTIC
PHILOSOPHY

WHAT chilly cloister or what lattice dim
Cast painted light upon this careful page?
What thought compulsive held the patient sage
Till sound of matin bell or evening hymn?
Did visions of the Heavenly Lover swim
Before his eyes in youth, or did stern rage
Against rash heresy keep green his age?
Had he seen God, to write so much of Him?
Gone is that irrecoverable mind
With all its phantoms, senseless to mankind
As a dream's trouble or the speech of birds.
The breath that stirred his lips he soon resigned
To windy chaos, and we only find
The garnered husks of his disusèd words.

ON THE DEATH OF A METAPHYSICIAN

UNHAPPY dreamer, who outwinged in flight
The pleasant region of the things I love,
And soared beyond the sunshine, and above
The golden cornfields and the dear and bright
Warmth of the hearth,—blasphemer of delight,
Was your proud bosom not at peace with Jove,
That you sought, thankless for his guarded grove,
The empty horror of abysmal night?
Ah, the thin air is cold above the moon!
I stood and saw you fall, befooled in death,
As, in your numbèd spirit's fatal swoon,
You cried you were a god, or were to be;
I heard with feeble moan your boastful breath
Bubble from depths of the Icarian sea.

ON A PIECE OF TAPESTRY

HOLD high the woof, dear friends, that we may see
The cunning mixture of its colours rare.
Nothing in nature purposely is fair,—
Her beauties in their freedom disagree;
But here all vivid dyes that garish be,
To that tint mellowed which the sense will bear,
Glow, and not wound the eye that, resting there,
Lingers to feed its gentle ecstasy.
Crimson and purple and all hues of wine,
Saffron and russet, brown and sober green
Are rich the shadowy depths of blue between;
While silver threads with golden intertwine,
To catch the glimmer of a fickle sheen,—
All the long labour of some captive queen.

TO W. P.

I

CALM was the sea to which your course you kept,
Oh, how much calmer than all southern seas!
Many your nameless mates, whom the keen breeze
Wafted from mothers that of old have wept.
All souls of children taken as they slept
Are your companions, partners of your ease,
And the green souls of all these autumn trees
Are with you through the silent spaces swept.
Your virgin body gave its gentle breath
Untainted to the gods. Why should we grieve,
But that we merit not your holy death?
We shall not loiter long, your friends and I;
Living you made it goodlier to live,
Dead you will make it easier to die.

II

WITH you a part of me hath passed away;
For in the peopled forest of my mind
A tree made leafless by this wintry wind
Shall never don again its green array.
Chapel and fireside, country road and bay,
Have something of their friendliness resigned;
Another, if I would, I could not find,
And I am grown much older in a day.
But yet I treasure in my memory
Your gift of charity, and young heart's ease,
And the dear honour of your amity;
For these once mine, my life is rich with these.
And I scarce know which part may greater be,—
What I keep of you, or you rob from me.

III

Your ship lies anchored in the peaceful bight
Until a kinder wind unfurl her sail;
Your docile spirit, wingèd by this gale,
Hath at the dawning fled into the light.
And I half know why heaven deemed it right
Your youth, and this my joy in youth, should fail;
God hath them still, for ever they avail,
Eternity hath borrowed that delight.
For long ago I taught my thoughts to run
Where all the great things live that lived of yore,
And in eternal quiet float and soar;
There all my loves are gathered into one,
Where change is not, nor parting any more,
Nor revolution of the moon and sun.

IV

In my deep heart these chimes would still have rung
To toll your passing, had you not been dead;
For time a sadder mask than death may spread
Over the face that ever should be young.
The bough that falls with all its trophies hung
Falls not too soon, but lays its flower-crowned head
Most royal in the dust, with no leaf shed
Unhallowed or unchiselled or unsung.
And though the after world will never hear
The happy name of one so gently true,
Nor chronicles write large this fatal year,
Yet we who loved you, though we be but few,
Keep you in whatsoe'er is good, and rear
In our weak virtues monuments to you.

BEFORE A STATUE OF ACHILLES

1

BEHOLD Pelides with his yellow hair,
Proud child of Thetis, hero loved of Jove;
Above the frowning of his brows it wove
A crown of gold, well combed, with Spartan care.
Who might have seen him, sullen, great, and fair,
As with the wrongful world he proudly strove,
And by high deeds his wilder passion shrove,
Mastering love, resentment, and despair.
He knew his end, and Phœbus' arrow sure
He braved for fame immortal and a friend,
Despising life; and we, who know our end,
Know that in our decay he shall endure
And all our children's hearts to grief inure,
With whose first bitter battles his shall blend.

II

Who brought thee forth, immortal vision, who
In Phthia or in Tempe brought thee forth?
Out of the sunlight and the sapful earth
What god the simples of thy spirit drew?
A goddess rose from the green waves, and threw
Her arms about a king, to give thee birth;
A centaur, patron of thy boyish mirth,
Over the meadows in thy footsteps flew.
Now Thessaly forgets thee, and the deep
Thy keeled bark furrowed answers not thy prayer;
But far away new generations keep
Thy laurels fresh, where branching Isis hems
The lawns of Oxford round about, or where
Enchanted Eton sits by pleasant Thames.

III

I GAZE on thee as Phidias of old
Or Polyclitus gazed, when first he saw
These hard and shining limbs, without a flaw,
And cast his wonder in heroic mould.
Unhappy me who only may behold,
Nor make immutable and fix in awe
A fair immortal form no worm shall gnaw,
A tempered mind whose faith was never told!
The godlike mien, the lion's lock and eye,
The well-knit sinew, utter a brave heart
Better than many words that part by part
Spell in strange symbols what serene and whole
In nature lives, nor can in marble die.
The perfect body is itself the soul.

THE RUSTIC AT THE PLAY

Our youth is like a rustic at the play
That cries aloud in simple-hearted fear,
Curses the villain, shudders at the fray,
And weeps before the maiden's wreathèd bier.
Yet once familiar with the changeful show,
He starts no longer at a brandished knife,
But, his heart chastened at the sight of woe,
Ponders the mirrored sorrows of his life.
So tutored too, I watch the moving art
Of all this magic and impassioned pain
That tells the story of the human heart
In a false instance, such as poets feign;
I smile, and keep within the parchment furled
That prompts the passions of this strutting world.

ODES

I

WHAT god will choose me from this labouring nation
To worship him afar, with inward gladness,
At sunset and at sunrise, in some Persian
       Garden of roses;

Or under the full moon, in rapturous silence,
Charmed by the trickling fountain, and the moaning
Of the death-hallowed cypress, and the myrtle
       Hallowed by Venus?

O for a chamber in an eastern tower,
Spacious and empty, roofed in odorous cedar,
A silken soft divan, a woven carpet
       Rich, many-coloured;

A jug that, poised on her firm head, a negress
Fetched from the well; a window to the ocean,
Lest of the stormy world too deep seclusion
       Make me forgetful!

Thence I might watch the vessel-bearing waters
Beat the slow pulses of the life eternal,
Bringing of nature's universal travail
       Infinite echoes;

And there at even I might stand and listen
To thrum of distant lutes and dying voices
Chanting the ditty an Arabian captive
       Sang to Darius.

So would I dream awhile, and ease a little
The soul long stifled and the straitened spirit,
Tasting new pleasures in a far-off country
       Sacred to beauty.

II

My heart rebels against my generation,
That talks of freedom and is slave to riches,
And, toiling 'neath each day's ignoble burden,
      Boasts of the morrow.

No space for noonday rest or midnight watches,
No purest joy of breathing under heaven!
Wretched themselves, they heap, to make them happy,
      Many possessions.

But thou, O silent Mother, wise, immortal,
To whom our toil is laughter,—take, divine one,
This vanity away, and to thy lover
      Give what is needful:—

A staunch heart, nobly calm, averse to evil,
The windy sky for breath, the sea, the mountain,
A well-born, gentle friend, his spirit's brother,
      Ever beside him.

What would you gain, ye seekers, with your striving,
Or what vast Babel raise you on your shoulders?
You multiply distresses, and your children
       Surely will curse you.

O leave them rather friendlier gods, and fairer
Orchards and temples, and a freer bosom!
What better comfort have we, or what other
       Profit in living,

Than to feed, sobered by the truth of Nature,
Awhile upon her bounty and her beauty,
And hand her torch of gladness to the ages
       Following after?

She hath not made us, like her other children,
Merely for peopling of her spacious kingdoms,
Beasts of the wild, or insects of the summer,
       Breeding and dying,

But also that we might, half knowing, worship
The deathless beauty of her guiding vision,
And learn to love, in all things mortal, only
       What is eternal.

III

GATHERING the echoes of forgotten wisdom,
And mastered by a proud, adventurous purpose,
Columbus sought the golden shores of India
        Opposite Europe.

He gave the world another world, and ruin
Brought upon blameless, river-loving nations,
Cursed Spain with barren gold, and made the Andes
        Fiefs of Saint Peter;

While in the cheerless North the thrifty Saxon
Planted his corn, and, narrowing his bosom,
Made covenant with God, and by keen virtue
        Trebled his riches.

What venture hast thou left us, bold Columbus?
What honour left thy brothers, brave Magellan?
Daily the children of the rich for pastime
        Circle the planet.

And what good comes to us of all your dangers?
A smaller earth and smaller hope of heaven.
Ye have but cheapened gold, and, measuring ocean,
      Counted the islands.

No Ponce de Leon shall drink in fountains,
On any flowering Easter, youth eternal;
No Cortes look upon another ocean;
      No Alexander

Found in the Orient dim a boundless kingdom,
And, clothing his Greek strength in barbarous splen-
   dour,
Build by the sea his throne, while sacred Egypt
      Honours his godhead.

The earth, the mother once of godlike Theseus
And mighty Heracles, at length is weary,
And now brings forth a spawn of antlike creatures,
      Blackening her valleys,

Inglorious in their birth and in their living,
Curious and querulous, afraid of battle,
Rummaging earth for coals, in camps of hovels
      Crouching from winter,

As if grim fate, amid our boastful prating,
Made us the image of our brutish fathers,
When from their caves they issued, crazed with terror,
      Howling and hungry.

For all things come about in sacred cycles,
And life brings death, and light eternal darkness,
And now the world grows old apace; its glory
       Passes for ever.

Perchance the earth will yet for many ages
Bear her dead child, her moon, around her orbit;
Strange craft may tempt the ocean streams, new forests
       Cover the mountains.

If in those latter days men still remember
Our wisdom and our travail and our sorrow,
They never can be happy, with that burden
       Heavy upon them,

Knowing the hideous past, the blood, the famine,
The ancestral hate, the eager faith's disaster,
All ending in their little lives, and vulgar
       Circle of troubles.

But if they have forgot us, and the shifting
Of sands has buried deep our thousand cities,
Fell superstition then will seize upon them;
       Protean error,

Will fill their panting heart with sickly phantoms
Of sudden blinding good and monstrous evil;
There will be miracles again, and torment,
       Dungeon, and fagot,—

Until the patient earth, made dry and barren,
Sheds all her herbage in a final winter,
And the gods turn their eyes to some far distant
Bright constellation.

Thine incense to the sun, thy gathered vapours,
He saw suspended on the flanks of Taurus,
Or veiling the snowed bosom of the virgin
            Sister of Atlas.

He saw the luminous top of wide Olympus,
Fit for the happy gods; he saw the pilgrim
River, with rains of Ethiopia flooding
            Populous Egypt.

And having seen, he loved thee.   His racked spirit,
By thy breath tempered and the light that clothes thee,
Forgot the monstrous gods, and made of Nature
            Mistress and mother.

The more should I, O fatal sea, before thee
Of alien words make echoes to thy music;
For I was born where first the rills of Tagus
            Turn to the westward,

And wandering long, alas! have need of drinking
Deep of the patience of thy perfect sadness,
O thou that constant through the change of ages,
            Beautiful ever,

Never wast wholly young and void of sorrows,
Nor ever canst be old, while yet the morning
Kindles thy ripples, or the golden evening
            Dyes thee in purple.

Thee, willing to be tamed but still untamable,
The Roman called his own until he perished,
As now the busy English hover o'er thee,
Stalwart and noble;

But all is naught to thee, while no harsh winter
Congeals thy fountains, and the blown Sahara
Chokes not with dreadful sand thy deep and placid
Rock-guarded havens.

Thou carest not what men may tread thy margin;
Nor I, while from some heather-scented headland
I may behold thy beauty, the eternal
Solace of mortals.

ATHLETIC ODE

I HEAR a rumour and a shout,
A louder heart-throb pulses in the air.
Fling, Muse, thy lattice open, and beware
    To keep the morning out.
Beckon into the chamber of thy care
        The bird of healing wing
        That trilleth there,
Blithe happy passion of the strong and fair.
Their wild heart singeth.   Do thou also sing.
            How vain, how vain
The feeble croaking of a reasoning tongue
        That heals no pain
And prompts no bright deed worthy to be sung!
        Too soon cold earth
Refuses flowers.   Oh, greet their lovely birth!
        Too soon dull death
Quiets the heaving of our doubtful breath.
        Deem not its worth
    Too high for honouring mirth;
    Sing while the lyre is strung,
And let the heart beat, while the heart is young.

When the dank earth begins to thaw and yield
The early clover, didst thou never pass
Some balmy noon from field to sunny field
And press thy feet against the tufted grass?
     So hadst thou seen
A spring palæstra on the tender green.
Here a tall stripling, with a woman's face,
Draws the spiked sandal on his upturned heel,
     Sure-footed for the race;
Another hurls the quoit of heavy steel
     And glories to be strong;
While yet another, lightest of the throng,
Crouching on tiptoe for the sudden bound,
Flies o'er the level race-course, like the hound,
     And soon is lost afar;
     Another jumps the bar,
For some god taught him easily to spring,
The legs drawn under, as a bird takes wing,
Till, tempting fortune farther than is meet,
At last he fails, and fails, and vainly tries,
And blushing, and ashamed to lift his eyes,
     Shakes the light earth from his feet.
     Him friendly plaudits greet
And pleasing to the unaccustomed ear.
Come then afield, come with the sporting year
     And watch the youth at play,
For gentle is the strengthening sun, and sweet
The soul of boyhood and the breath of May.

And with the milder ray
Of the declining sun, when sky and shore,
In purple drest and misty silver-grey,
    Hang curtains round the day,
Come list the beating of the plashing oar,
For grief in rhythmic labour glides away.
The glancing blades make circles where they dip,—
    Now flash and drip
Cool wind-blown drops into the glassy river,
    Now sink and cleave,
    While the lithe rowers heave
And feel the boat beneath them leap and quiver.
    The supple oars in time,
Shattering the mirror of the rippled water,
    Fly, fly as poets climb,
Borne by the pliant promise of their rhyme,
Or as bewitched by Nereus' loveliest daughter
The painted dolphins, following along,
Leap to the measure of her liquid song.

    But the blasts of late October,
    Tempering summer's paling grief
    With a russet glow and sober,
Bring of these sports the latest and the chief.
Then bursts the flame from many a smouldering ember,
    And many an ardent boy
Woos harsher pleasures sweeter to remember,
Hugged with a sterner and a tenser joy.
    Look where the rivals come:

Each little phalanx on its chosen ground
Strains for the sudden shock, and all around
    The multitude is dumb.
    Come, watch the stubborn fight
    And doubtful, in the sight
Of wide-eyed beauty and unstinted love,
    Ay, the wise gods above,
Attentive to this hot and generous fray,
Smile on its fortunes and its end prepare,
For play is also life, and far from care
    Their own glad life is play.

Ye nymphs and fauns, to Bacchus dear,
That woke Cithæron with your midnight rout,
    Arise, arise and shout!
Your day returns, your haunt is here.
Shake off dull sleep and long despair;
There is intoxication in this air,
And frenzy in this yelping cheer.
How oft of old the enraptured Muses sung
    Olympian victors' praise.
    Lo! even in these days
    The world is young.
    Life like a torrent flung
    For ever down
For ever wears a rainbow for a crown.
O idle sigh for loveliness outworn,
When the red flush of each unfailing morn
    Floods every field and grove,

And no moon wanes but some one is in love.
   O wasted tear,
A new soul wakes with each awakened year.
Beneath these rags, these blood-clots on the face,
The valiant soul is still the same, the same
The strength, the art, the inevitable grace,
   The thirst unquenched for fame
Quenching base passion, the high will severe,
The long obedience, and the knightly flame
Of loyalty to honour and a name.

Give o'er, ye chords, your music ere ye tire,
   Be sweetly mute, O lyre.
Words soon are cold, and life is warm for ever.
One half of honour is the strong endeavour,
Success the other, but when both conspire
Youth has her perfect crown, and age her old desire.

VARIOUS POEMS

CAPE COD

THE low sandy beach and the thin scrub pine,
The wide reach of bay and the long sky line,—
    O, I am far from home!

The salt, salt smell of the thick sea air,
And the smooth round stones that the ebbtides wear,—
    When will the good ship come?

The wretched stumps all charred and burned,
And the deep soft rut where the cartwheel turned,—
    Why is the world so old?

The lapping wave, and the broad gray sky
Where the cawing crows and the slow gulls fly,—
    Where are the dead untold?

The thin, slant willows by the flooded bog,
The huge stranded hulk and the floating log,—
    Sorrow with life began!

And among the dark pines, and along the flat shore,
O the wind, and the wind, for evermore!
    What will become of man?

A TOAST

SEE this bowl of purple wine,
Life-blood of the lusty vine!
All the warmth of summer suns
In the vintage liquid runs,
All the glow of winter nights
Plays about its jewel lights,
Thoughts of time when love was young
Lurk its ruby drops among,
And its deepest depths are dyed
With delight of friendship tried.
Worthy offering, I ween,
For a god or for a queen,
Is the draught I pour to thee,—
Comfort of all misery,
Single friend of the forlorn,
Haven of all beings born,
Hope when trouble wakes at night,
And when naught delights, delight.
Holy Death, I drink to thee;
Do not part my friends and me.
Take this gift, which for a night
Puts dull leaden care to flight,
Thou who takest grief away
For a night and for a day.

PREMONITION

THE muffled syllables that Nature speaks
    Fill us with deeper longing for her word;
She hides a meaning that the spirit seeks,
    She makes a sweeter music than is heard.

A hidden light illumines all our seeing,
    An unknown love enchants our solitude,
We feel and know that from the depths of being
    Exhales an infinite, a perfect good.

Though the heart wear the garment of its sorrow
    And be not happy like a naked star,
Yet from the thought of peace some peace we borrow,
    Some rapture from the rapture felt afar.

Our heart strings are too coarse for Nature's fingers
    Deftly to quicken as she pulses on,
And the harsh tremor that among them lingers
    Will into sweeter silence die anon.

We catch the broken prelude and suggestion
  Of things unuttered, needing to be sung;
We know the burden of them, and their question
  Lies heavy on the heart, nor finds a tongue.

Till haply, lightning through the storm of ages,
  Our sullen secret flash from sky to sky,
Glowing in some diviner poet's pages
  And swelling into rapture from this sigh.

SOLIPSISM

I COULD believe that I am here alone,
   And all the world my dream;
The passion of the scene is all my own,
   And things that seem but seem.

Perchance an exhalation of my sorrow
   Hath raised this vaporous show,
For whence but from my soul should all things borrow
   So deep a tinge of woe?

I keep the secret doubt within my breast
   To be the gods' defence,
To ease the heart by too much ruth oppressed
   And drive the horror hence.

O sorrow that the patient brute should cower
   And die, not having sinned!
O pity that the wild and fragile flower
   Should shiver in the wind!

Then were I dreaming dreams I know not of,
    For that is part of me
That feels the piercing pang of grief and love
    And doubts eternally.

But whether all to me the vision come
    Or break in many beams,
The pageant ever shifts, and being's sum
    Is but the sum of dreams.

SYBARIS

Lap, ripple, lap, Icarian wave, the sand
Along the ruins of this piteous land;
Murmur the praises of a lost delight,
And soothe the aching of my starvèd sight
With sheen of mirrored beauties, caught aright.

Here stood enchanted palaces of old,
All veinèd porphyry and burnished gold;
Here matrons and slight maidens sat aloof
Beneath cool porches, rich with Tyrian woof
Hung from the carven rafters of the roof.

Here in a mart a swarthy turbaned brave
Showed the wrought blade or praised the naked slave.
"Touch with your finger-tips this edge of steel,"
Quoth he, "and see this lad, from head to heel
Like a bronze Cupid.   Feel, my masters, feel."

Here Aphrodite filled with frenzied love
The dark recesses of her murmurous grove.
The doves that haunted it, the winds that sighed,

Were souls of youths that in her coverts died,
And hopes of heroes strewed her garden wide.

Under her shades a narrow brazen gate
Led to the courts of Ares and of Fate.
Who entered breathed the unutterable prayer
Of cruel hearts, and death was worshipped there,
And men went thence enfranchised by despair.

Here the proud athlete in the baths delayed,
While a cool fountain on his shoulders played,
Then in fine linen swathed his breast and thighs,
And silent, myrtle crowned, with serious eyes,
Stepped forth to list the wranglings of the wise.

A sage stalked by, his ragged mantle bound
About his brows; his eyes perused the ground;
He conned the number of the cube and square
Of the moon's orb; his horny feet and bare
Trampled the lilies carpeting the stair.

A jasper terrace hung above the sea
Where the King supped with his belovèd three:
The Libyan chanted of her native land
In raucous melody, the Indian fanned,
And the huge mastiff licked his master's hand.

Below, alone, despairing of the gale,
A crouching sailor furled the saffron sail;

Then rose, breathed deep, and plunged in the lagoon.
A mermaid spied his glistening limbs: her croon
Enticed him down; her cold arms choked him soon.

And the King laughed, filled full his jewelled bowl,
And drinking mused: "What know we of the soul?
What magic, perfecting her harmony,
Have these red drops that so attune her key,
Or those of brine that set the wretched free?

"If death should change me, as old fables feign,
Into some slave or beast, to purge with pain
My lordly pleasures, let my torment be
Still to behold thee, Sybaris, and see
The sacred horror of thy loves and thee.

"Be thou my hell, my dumb eternal grief,
But spare thy King the madness of belief,
The brutish faith of ignorant desire
That strives and wanders. Let the visible fire
Of beauty torture me. That doom is higher.

"I wear the crown of life. The rose and gem
Twine with the pale gold of my diadem.
Nature, long secret, hath unveiled to me
And proved her vile. Her wanton bosoms be
My pillow now. I know her, I am free."

He spoke, and smiling stretched a languid hand,
And music burst in mighty chords and bland
Of harp and flute and cymbal.—When between
Two cypresses the large moon rose, her sheen
Silvered the nymphs' feet, tripping o'er the green.

AVILA

AGAIN my feet are on the fragrant moor
   Amid the purple uplands of Castile,
Realm proudly desolate and nobly poor,
   Scorched by the sky's inexorable zeal.

Wide desert where a diadem of towers
   Above Adaja hems a silent town,
And locks, unmindful of the mocking hours,
   Her twenty temples in a granite crown.

The shafts of fervid light are in the sky,
   And in my heart the mysteries of yore.
Here the sad trophies of my spirit lie:
   These dead fulfilled my destiny before.

Like huge primeval stones that strew this plain,
   Their nameless sorrows sink upon my breast,
And like this ardent sky their cancelled pain
   Smiles at my grief and quiets my unrest.

For here hath mortal life from age to age
   Endured the silent hand that makes and mars,
And, sighing, taken up its heritage
   Beneath the smiling and inhuman stars.

Still o'er this town the crested castle stands,
   A nest for storks, as once for haughty souls,
Still from the abbey, where the vale expands,
   The curfew for the long departed tolls,

Wafting some ghostly blessing to the heart
   From prayer of nun or silent Capuchin,
To heal with balm of Golgotha the smart
   Of weary labour and distracted sin.

What fate has cast me on a tide of time
   Careless of joy and covetous of gold,
What force compelled to weave the pensive rhyme
   When loves are mean, and faith and honour old,

When riches crown in vain men's sordid lives,
   And learning chokes a mind of base degree?
What wingèd spirit rises from their hives?
   What heart, revolting, ventures to be free?

Their pride will sink and more ignobly fade
   Without memorial of its hectic fire.
What altars shall survive them, where they prayed?
   What lovely deities?   What riven lyre?

Tarry not, pilgrim, but with inward gaze
    Pass daily, musing, where their prisons are,
And o'er the ocean of their babble raise
    Thy voice in greeting to thy changeless star.

Abroad a tumult, and a ruin here;
    Nor world nor desert hath a home for thee.
Out of the sorrows of the barren year
    Build thou thy dwelling in eternity.

Let patience, faith's wise sister, be thy heaven,
    And with high thoughts necessity alloy.
Love is enough, and love is ever given,
    While fleeting days bring gift of fleeting joy.

The little pleasures that to catch the sun
    Bubble a moment up from being's deep,
The glittering sands of passion as they run,
    The merry laughter and the happy sleep,—

These are the gems that, like the stars on fire,
    Encrust with glory all our heaven's zones;
Each shining atom, in itself entire,
    Brightens the galaxy of sister stones,

Dust of a world that crumbled when God's dream
    To throbbing pulses broke the life of things,
And mingled with the void the scattered gleam
    Of many orbs that move in many rings,

Perchance at last into the parent sun
  To fall again and reunite their rays,
When God awakes and gathers into one
  The light of all his loves and all his days.

KING'S COLLEGE CHAPEL

THE buttress frowns, the gorgeous windows blaze,
   The vaults hang wonderful with woven fans,
The four stone sentinels to heaven raise
   Their heads, in a more constant faith than man's.

The College gathers, and the courtly prayer
   Is answered still by hymn and organ-groan;
The beauty and the mystery are there,
   The Virgin and Saint Nicholas are gone.

Not one *Ora pro nobis* bids them pause
   In their far flight, to hear this anthem roll;
No heart, of all that the King's relic awes,
   Sings *Requiescat* to his mournful soul.

No grain of incense thrown upon the embers
   Of their cold hearth, no lamp in witness hung
Before their image. One alone remembers;
   Only the stranger knows their mother tongue.

Long rows of tapers light the people's places;
  The little choristers may read, and mark
The rhythmic fall; I see their wondering faces;
  Only the altar—like the soul—is dark.

Ye floating voices through these arches ringing
  With measured music, subtle, sweet, and strong,
Feel ye the inmost reason of your singing?
  Know ye the ancient burden of your song?

The twilight deepens, and the blood-dyed glories
  Of all these fiery blazonings are dim.
Oh, they are jumbled, sad, forgotten stories!
  Why should ye read them, children? Chant your
    hymn.

But I must con them while the rays of even
  Kindle aloft some fading jewel-gleam
And the vast windows glow a peopled heaven,
  Rich with the gathering pageant of my dream.

Eden I see, where from the leafy cover
  The green-eyed snake begins to uncoil his length
And whispers to the woman and her lover,
  As they lie musing, large, in peaceful strength.

I see their children, bent with toil and terror,
  Lurking in caves, or heaping madly on
The stones of Babel, or the endless error
  Of Sodom, Nineveh, and Babylon.

Here the Egyptian, wedding life with death,
　　Flies from the sun into his painted tomb,
And winds the secret of his antique faith
　　Tight in his shroud, and seals in sterile gloom.

There the bold prophets of the heart's desire
　　Hail the new Zion God shall build for them,
And rapt Isaiah strikes the heavenly lyre,
　　And Jeremiah mourns Jerusalem.

Here David's daughter, full of grace and truth,
　　Kneels in the temple, waiting for the Lord;
With the first *Ave* comes the wingèd youth,
　　Bringing the lily ere he bring the sword.

There, to behold the Mother and the Child,
　　The sturdy shepherds down the mountain plod,
And angels sing, with voices sweet and wild
　　And wide lips parted: "Glory be to God."

Here, mounted on an ass, the twain depart
　　To hallowed Egypt, safe from Herod's wrong;
And Mary ponders all things in her heart,
　　And pensive Joseph sadly walks along.

There with the Twelve, before his blood is shed,
　　Christ blesses bread and breaks it with his hands,
"This is my body."　Thomas shakes his head,
　　They marvel all, and no one understands,

Save John, whom Jesus loved above the rest.
    He marvels too, but, seeking naught beside,
Leans, as his wont is, on his Master's breast.
    Ah! the Lord's body also should abide.

There Golgotha is dark against the blue
    In the broad east, above the painted crowd,
And many look upon the sign, but few
    Read the hard lesson of the cross aloud.

And from this altar, now an empty tomb,
    The Lord is risen. Lo! he is not here.
No shining angel sitteth in the gloom
    No Magdalen in anguish draweth near.

All pure in heart, or all in aspect pure,
    The seemly Christians, kneeling, line the choir,
And drop their eyelids, tender and demure,
    As the low lingering harmonies expire.

In that *Amen* are the last echoes blended
    Of all the ghostly world. The shades depart
Into the sacred night. In peace is ended
    The long delirious fever of the heart.

Then I go forth into the open wold
    And breathe the vigour of the freshening wind,
And with the piling drift of cloud I hold
    A worship sweeter to the homeless mind,

Where the squat willows with their osiers crowned
    Border the humble reaches of the Cam,
And the deep meadows stretching far around
    Make me forget the exile that I am,—

Exile not only from the wind-swept moor
    Where Guadarrama lifts his purple crest,
But from the spirit's realm, celestial, sure
    Goal of all hope and vision of the best.

They also will go forth, these gentle youths,
    Strong in the virtues of their manful isle,
Till one the pathway of the forest smooths,
    And one the Ganges rules, and one the Nile;

And to whatever wilderness they choose
    Their hearts will bear the sanctities of home,
The perfect ardours of the Grecian Muse,
    The mighty labour of the arms of Rome;

But, ah! how little of these storied walls
    Beneath whose shadow all their nurture was!
No, not one passing memory recalls
    The Blessed Mary and Saint Nicholas.

Unhappy King, look not upon these towers,
    Remember not thine only work that grew.
The moving world that feeds thy gift devours,
    And the same hand that finished overthrew.

ON AN UNFINISHED STATUE

BY MICHAEL ANGELO IN THE BARGELLO, CALLED AN
APOLLO OR A DAVID

WHAT beauteous form beneath a marble veil
  Awaited in this block the Master's hand?
Could not the magic of his art avail
  To unseal that beauty's tomb and bid it stand?

Alas! the torpid and unwilling mass
  Misknew the sweetness of the mind's control,
And the quick shifting of the winds, alas!
  Denied a body to that flickering soul.

Fair homeless spirit, harbinger of bliss,
  It wooed dead matter that they both might live,
But dreamful earth still slumbered through the kiss
  And missed the blessing heaven stooped to give,

As when Endymion, locked in dullard sleep,
  Endured the gaze of Dian, till she turned
Stung with immortal wrath and doomed to weep
  Her maiden passion ignorantly spurned.

How should the vision stay to guide the hand,
   How should the holy thought and ardour stay,
When the false deeps of all the soul are sand
   And the loose rivets of the spirit clay?

What chisel shaking in the pulse of lust
   Shall find the perfect line, immortal, pure?
What fancy blown by every random gust
   Shall mount the breathless heavens and endure?

Vain was the trance through which a thrill of joy
   Passed for the nonce, when a vague hand, unled,
Half shaped the image of this lovely boy
   And caught the angel's garment as he fled.

Leave, leave, distracted hand, the baffling stone,
   And on that clay, thy fickle heart, begin.
Mould first some steadfast virtue of thine own
   Out of the sodden substance of thy sin.

They who wrought wonders by the Nile of old,
   Bequeathing their immortal part to us,
Cast their own spirit first into the mould
   And were themselves the rock they fashioned thus.

Ever their docile and unwearied eye
   Traced the same ancient pageant to the grave,
And awe made rich their spirit's husbandry
   With the perpetual refluence of its wave,

III

Till 'twixt the desert and the constant Nile
    Sphinx, pyramid, and awful temple grew,
And the vast gods, self-knowing, learned to smile
    Beneath the sky's unalterable blue.

Long, long ere first the rapt Arcadian swain
    Heard Pan's wild music pulsing through the grove,
His people's shepherds held paternal reign
    Beneath the large benignity of Jove.

Long mused the Delphic sibyl in her cave
    Ere mid his laurels she beheld the god,
And Beauty rose a virgin from the wave
    In lands the foot of Heracles had trod.

Athena reared her consecrated wall,
    Poseidon laid its rocky basement sure,
When Theseus had the monstrous race in thrall
    And made the worship of his people pure.

Long had the stripling stood in silence, veiled,
    Hearing the heroes' legend o'er and o'er,
Long in the keen palæstra striven, nor quailed
    To tame the body to the task it bore,

Ere soul and body, shaped by patient art,
    Walked linkèd with the gods, like friend with friend,
And reason, mirrored in the sage's heart,
    Beheld her purpose and confessed her end.

Mould, then, thyself and let the marble be.
  Look not to frailty for immortal themes,
Nor mock the travail of mortality
  With barren husks and harvesting of dreams.

MIDNIGHT

THE dank earth reeks with three days' rain,
The phantom trees are dark and still,
Above the darkness and the hill
The tardy moon shines out again.
O heavy lethargy of pain!
O shadows of forgotten ill!

My parrot lips, when I was young,
To prove and to disprove were bold.
The mighty world has tied my tongue,
And in dull custom growing old
I leave the burning truth untold
And the heart's anguish all unsung.

Youth dies in man's benumbèd soul,
Maid bows to woman's broken life,
A thousand leagues of silence roll
Between the husband and the wife.
The spirit faints with inward strife
And lonely gazing at the pole.

But how should reptiles pine for wings
Or a parched desert know its dearth?
Immortal is the soul that sings
The sorrow of her mortal birth.
O cruel beauty of the earth!
O love's unutterable stings!

IN GRANTCHESTER MEADOWS

ON FIRST HEARING A SKYLARK SING

Too late, thou tender songster of the sky
Trilling unseen, by things unseen inspired,
      I list thy far-heard cry
That poets oft to kindred song hath fired,
As floating through the purple veils of air
      Thy soul is poured on high,
A little joy in an immense despair.

Too late thou biddest me escape the earth,
      In ignorance of wrong
To spin a little slender thread of song;
      On yet unwearied wing
      To rise and soar and sing,
      Not knowing death or birth
Or any true unhappy human thing.

      To dwell 'twixt field and cloud,
By river-willow and the murmurous sedge,
      Be thy sweet privilege,

To thee and to thy happy lords allowed.
My native valley higher mountains hedge
　　　'Neath starlit skies and proud,
And sadder music in my soul is loud.

　　　Yet have I loved thy voice,
Frail echo of some ancient sacred joy.
　　　Ah, who might not rejoice
Here to have wandered, a fair English boy,
And breathed with life thy rapture and thy rest
Where woven meadow-grasses fold thy nest?
　　　But whose life is his choice?
And he who chooseth not hath chosen best.

SPAIN IN AMERICA

WRITTEN AFTER THE DESTRUCTION OF THE SPANISH
FLEET IN THE BATTLE OF SANTIAGO, IN 1898

I

WHEN scarce the echoes of Manila Bay,
Circling each slumbering billowy hemisphere,
Had met where Spain's forlorn Armada lay
Locked amid hostile hills, and whispered near
The double omen of that groan and cheer—
Haste to do now what must be done anon
Or some mad hope of selling triumph dear
Drove the ships forth: soon was *Teresa* gone,
Furór, Plutón, Vizcaya, Oquendo, and *Colón.*

And when the second morning dawned serene
O'er vivid waves and foam-fringed mountains,
    dressed
Like Nessus in their robe's envenomed sheen,
Scarce by some fiery fleck the place was guessed
Where each hulk smouldered; while from crest **to**
    crest

Leapt through the North the news of victory,
Victory tarnished by a boorish jest [1]
Yet touched with pity, lest the unkindly sea
Should too much aid the strong and leave no enemy.

As the anguished soul, that gasped for difficult
    breath,
Passes to silence from its house of pain,
So from those wrecks, in fumes of lurid death,
Passed into peace the heavy pride of Spain,
Passed from that aching tenement, half fain,
Back to her castled hills and windy moors,
No longer tossed upon the treacherous main
Once boasted hers, which with its watery lures
Too long enticed her sons to unhallowed sepultures.

II

WHY went Columbus to that highland race,
Frugal and pensive, prone to love and ire,
Despising kingdoms for a woman's face,
For honour, riches and for faith desire?
On Spain's own breast was snow, within it fire;
In her own eyes and subtle tongue was mirth;
The eternal brooded in her skies, whence nigher
The trebled starry host admonished earth
To shame away her grief and mock her baubles' worth.

[1] Admiral Sampson said he made a Fourth of July present of the
Spanish fleet to the American people, although all the ships had
been sunk and none captured.

Ah! when the crafty Tyrian came to Spain
To barter for her gold his motley wares,
Treading her beaches he forgot his gain.
The Semite became noble unawares.
Her passion breathed Hamilcar's cruel prayers;
Her fiery winds taught Hannibal his vows;
Out of her tribulations and despairs
They wove a sterile garland for their brows.
To her sad ports they fled before the Roman prows.

And the Greek coming too forgot his art,
And that large temperance which made him wise.
The wonder of her mountains choked his heart,
The languor of her gardens veiled his eyes;
He dreamed, he doubted; in her deeper skies
He read unfathomed oracles of woe,
And stubborn to the onward destinies,
Like some dumb brute before a human foe,
Sank in Saguntum's flames and deemed them brighter
        so.

The mighty Roman also when he came,
Bringing his gods, his justice, and his tongue,
Put off his greatness for a sadder fame,
And what a Cæsar wrought a Lucan sung.
Nor was the pomp of his proud music, wrung
From Latin numbers, half so stern and dire,
Nor the sad majesties he moved among

Half so divine, as her unbreathed desire.
Shall longing break the heart and not untune the lyre?

When after many conquerors came Christ,
The only conqueror of Spain indeed,
Not Bethlehem nor Golgotha sufficed
To show him forth, but every shrine must bleed
And every shephered in his watches heed
The angels' matins sung at heaven's gate.
Nor seemed the Virgin Mother wholly freed
From taint of ill if born in frail estate,
But shone the seraphs' queen and soared immaculate.

And when the Arab from his burning sands
Swept o'er the waters like a heavenly flail,
He took her lute into his conquering hands,
And in her midnight turned to nightingale.
With woven lattices and pillars frail
He screened the pleasant secrets of his bower,
Yet little could his subtler arts avail
Against the brutal onset of the Giaour.
The rose passed from his courts, the muezzin from his
    tower.

Only one image of his wisdom stayed,
One only relic of his magic lore,—
Allah the Great, whom silent fate obeyed,
More than Jehovah calm and hidden more,
Allah remained in her heart's kindred core

High witness of these terrene shifts of wrong.
Into his ancient silence she could pour
Her passions' frailty—He alone is strong—
And chant with lingering wail the burden of her song.

Seizing at Covadonga the rude cross
Pelayo raised amid his mountaineers,
She bore it to Granada, one day's loss
Ransomed with battles of a thousand years.
A nation born in harness, fed on tears,
Christened in blood, and schooled in sacrifice,
All for a sweeter music in the spheres,
All for a painted heaven—at a price
Should she forsake her loves and sail to Ind for spice?

Had Genoa in her merchant palaces
No welcome for a heaven-guided son?
Had Venice, mistress of the inland seas,
No ships for bolder venture? Pisa none?
Was sated Rome content? Her mission done?
Saw Lusitania in her seaward dreams
No floating premonition, beckoning on
To vast horizons, gilded yet with gleams
Of old Atlantis, whelmed beneath the bubbling
    streams?

Or if some torpor lay upon the South,
Tranced by the might of memories divine,
Dwelt no shrewd princeling by the marshy mouth

Of Scheldt, or by the many mouths of Rhine?
Rode Albion not at anchor in the brine
Whose throne but now the thrifty Tudor stole
Changing a noble for a crafty line?
Swarmed not the Norsemen yet about the pole,
Seeking through endless mists new havens for the
    soul?

These should have been thy mates, Columbus,
    these
Patrons and partners of thy enterprise,
Sad lovers of immeasurable seas,
Bound to no hallowed earth, no peopled skies.
No ray should reach them of their ladies' eyes
In western deserts: no pure minstrel's rhyme,
Echoing in forest solitudes, surprise
Their heart with longing for a sweeter clime.
These, these should found a world who drag no chains
    of time.

In sooth it had seemed folly, to reveal
To stubborn Aragon and evil-eyed
These perilous hopes, folly to dull Castile
Moated in jealous faith and walled in pride,
Save that those thoughts, to Spain's fresh deeds
    allied,
Painted new Christian conquests, and her hand
Itched for that sword, now dangling at her side,

Which drove the Moslem forth and purged the
    land.
And then she dreamed a dream her heart could
    understand.

III

THREE caravels, a cross upon the prow,
A broad cross on the banner and the sail,
The liquid fields of Hesperus should plough
Borne by the leaping waters and the gale.
Before that sign all hellish powers should quail
Troubling the deep: no dragon's obscene crest,
No serpent's slimy coils should aught avail,
Till ivory cities looming in the west
Should gleam from high Cathay or Araby the Blest.

Then, as with noble mien and debonair
The captains from the galleys leapt to land,
Or down the temple's alabaster stair
Or by the river's marge of silvery sand,
Proud Sultans should descend with outstretched
    hand
Greeting the strangers, and by them apprised
Of Christ's redemption and the Queen's command,
Being with joy and gratitude baptized,
Should lavish gifts of price by rarest art devised.

Or if (since churls there be) they should demur
To some least point of fealty or faith,
A champion, clad in arms from crest to spur,
Should challenge the proud caitiffs to their death
And, singly felling them, from their last breath
Extort confession that the Lord is lord,
And India's Catholic queen, Elizabeth.
Whereat yon turbaned tribes, with one accord,
Should beat their heathen breasts and ope their
    treasures' hoard.

Or, if the worst should chance and high debates
Should end in insult and outrageous deed,
And, many Christians rudely slain, their mates
Should summon heaven to their direful need,
Suddenly from the clouds a snow-white steed
Bearing a dazzling rider clad in flames
Should plunge into the fray: with instant speed
Rout all the foe at once, while mid acclaims
The slaughtered braves should rise, crying, *Saint
    James! Saint James!*

Then, the day won, and its bright arbiter
Vanished, save for peace he left behind,
Each in his private bosom should bestir
His dearest dream: as that perchance there pined
Some lovely maiden of angelic mind
In those dark towers, awaiting out of Spain
Two Saviours that her horoscope divined

125

Should thence arrive.   She (womanlike) were fain
Not to be wholly free, but wear a chosen chain.

That should be youth's adventure.   Riper days
Would crave the guerdon of a prouder power
And pluck their nuggets from an earthly maze
For rule and dignity and children's dower.
And age that thought to near the fatal hour
Should to a magic fount descend instead,
Whose waters with the fruit revive the flower
And deck in all its bloom the ashen head,
Where a green heaven spreads, not peopled of the
    dead.

IV

By such false meteors did those helmsmen steer,
Such phantoms filled their vain and vaulting souls
With divers ardours, while this brooding sphere
Swung yet ungirdled on her silent poles.
All journeys took them farther from their goals,
All battles won defeated their desire,
Barred from one India by the other's shoals,
Each sighted star extinguishing its fire,
Cape doubled after cape, and never haven nigher.

How many galleons sailed to sail no more,
How many battles and how many slain,
Since first Columbus touched the Cuban shore,

126

Till Araucania felt the yoke of Spain!
What mounting miseries! What dwindling gain!
To till those solitudes, soon swept of gold,
And bear that ardent sun, across the main
Slaves must come writhing in the festering hold
Of galleys.—Poison works, though men be brave
      and bold.

That slothful planter, once the buccaneer,
Lord of his bastards and his mongrel clan,
Ignorant, harsh, what could he list or hear
Of Europe and the heritage of man?
No petty schemer sees the larger plan,
No privy tyrant brooks the mightier law,
But lash in hand rides forth a partisan
Of freedom: base, without the touch of awe,
He poisoned first the blood his poniard was to draw.

By sloth and lust and mindlessness and pelf
Spain sank in sadness and dishonour down,
Each in his service serving but himself,
Each in his passion striking at her crown.
Not that these treasons blotted her renown
Emblazoned higher than such hands can reach:
There where she reaped but sorrow she has sown
The balm of sorrow; all she had to teach
She taught the younger world—her faith and heart
      and speech.

And now within her sea-girt walls withdrawn
She waits in silence for the healing years,
While where her sun has set a second dawn
Comes from the north, with other hopes and fears.
Spain's daughters stand, half ceasing from their
    tears,
And watch the skies from Cuba to the Horn.
"What is this dove or eagle that appears,"
They seem to cry, "what herald of what morn
Hovers o'er Andes' peaks in love or guile or scorn?"

"O brooding Spirit, fledgling of the North,
Winged for the levels of its shifting light,
Child of a labouring ocean and an earth
Shrouded in vapours, fear the southward flight,
Dread waveless waters and their warm delight,
Beware of peaks that cleave the cloudless blue
And hold communion with the naked night.
The souls went never back that hither flew,
But sighing fell to earth or broke the heavens through.

"Haunt still thy storm-swept islands, and endure
The shimmering forest where thy visions live.
Then if we love thee—for thy heart is pure—
Thou shalt have something worthy love to give.
Thrust not thy prophets on us, nor believe
Thy sorry riches in our eyes are fair.
Thy unctuous sophists never will deceive

A mortal pang, or charm away despair.
Not for the stranger's fee we plait our lustrous hair.

"But of thy lingering twilight bring some gleam,
Memorial of the immaterial fire
Lighting thy heart, and to a wider dream
Waken the music of our plaintive lyre.
Check our rash word, hush, hush our base desire.
Hang paler clouds of reverence about
Our garish skies: laborious hope inspire
That uncomplaining walks the paths of doubt,
A wistful heart within, a mailèd breast without.

"Gold found is dross, but long Promethean art
Transmutes to gold the unprofitable ore.
Bring labour's joy, yet spare that better part
Our mother, Spain, bequeathed to all she bore,
For who shall covet if he once adore?
Leave in our skies, strange Spirit passing there,
No less of vision but of courage more,
And of our worship take thy equal share,
Thou who wouldst teach us hope, with her who
taught us prayer."

A MINUET

I

Old Age, on tiptoe, lays her jewelled hand
Lightly in mine.—Come, tread a stately measure,
Most gracious partner, nobly poised and bland.
　　　Ours be no boisterous pleasure,
But smiling conversation, with quick glance
And memories dancing lightlier than we dance,
　　　Friends who a thousand joys
Divide and double, save one joy supreme
　　　Which many a pang alloys.
　　　Let wanton girls and boys
Cry over lovers' woes and broken toys.
Our waking life is sweeter than their dream.

II

Dame Nature, with unwitting hand,
Has sparsely strewn the black abyss with lights

130

Minute, remote, and numberless. We stand
    Measuring far depths and heights,
    Arched over by a laughing heaven,
Intangible and never to be scaled.
If we confess our sins, they are forgiven.
    We triumph, if we know we failed.

III

    Tears that in youth you shed,
Congealed to pearls, now deck your silvery hair;
    Sighs breathed for loves long dead
Frosted the glittering atoms of the air
    Into the veils you wear
Round your soft bosom and most queenly head;
    The shimmer of your gown
Catches all tints of autumn, and the dew
Of gardens where the damask roses blew;
The myriad tapers from these arches hung
    Play on your diamonded crown;
And stars, whose light angelical caressed
    Your virgin days,
Give back in your calm eyes their holier rays.
    The deep past living in your breast
    Heaves these half-merry sighs;
    And the soft accents of your tongue
    Breathe unrecorded charities.

IV

Hasten not; the feast will wait.
This is a master-night without a morrow.
No chill and haggard dawn, with after-sorrow,
  Will snuff the spluttering candle out,
Or blanch the revellers homeward straggling late.
  Before the rout
Wearies or wanes, will come a calmer trance.
Lulled by the poppied fragrance of this bower,
  We'll cheat the lapsing hour,
And close our eyes, still smiling, on the dance.

December 1913.

132

TRANSLATIONS

FROM MICHAEL ANGELO

I

"Non so se s'è la desiata luce"

I KNOW not if from uncreated spheres
Some longed-for ray it be that warms my breast,
Or lesser light, in memory expressed,
Of some once lovely face, that reappears,
Or passing rumour ringing in my ears,
Or dreamy vision, once my bosom's guest,
That left behind I know not what unrest,
Haply the reason of these wayward tears.
But what I feel and seek, what leads me on,
Comes not of me; nor can I tell aright
Where shines the hidden star that sheds this light.
Since I beheld thee, sweet and bitter fight
Within me.   Resolution have I none.
Can this be, Master, what thine eyes have done?

II

THE haven and last refuge of my pain
(A safe and strong defence)
Are tears and supplications, but in vain.
Love sets upon me banded with Disdain,
One armed with pity and one armed with death,
And as death smites me, pity lends me breath.
Else had my soul long since departed thence.
She pineth to remove
Whither her hopes of endless peace abide
And beauty dwelleth without beauty's pride,
There her last bliss to prove.
But still the living fountain of her tears
Wells in the heart when all thy truth appears,
Lest death should vanquish love.

III

"Gli occhi miei vaghi delle cose belle"

RAVISHED by all that to the eyes is fair,
Yet hungry for the joys that truly bless,
My soul can find no stair
To mount to heaven, save earth's loveliness.
For from the stars above
Descends a glorious light
That lifts our longing to their highest height
And bears the name of love.
Nor is there aught can move
A gentle heart, or purge or make it wise,
But beauty and the starlight of her eyes.

FROM THEOPHILE GAUTIER

ART

ALL things are doubly fair
If patience fashion them
And care—
Verse, enamel, marble, gem.

No idle chains endure:
Yet, Muse, to walk aright,
Lace tight
Thy buskin proud and sure.

Fie on a facile measure,
A shoe where every lout
At pleasure
Slips his foot in and out!

Sculptor, lay by the clay
On which thy nerveless finger
May linger,
Thy thoughts flown far away.

Keep to Carrara rare,
Struggle with Paros cold,
        That hold
The subtle line and fair.

Lest haply nature lose
That proud, that perfect line,
        Make thine
The bronze of Syracuse.

And with a tender dread
Upon an agate's face
        Retrace
Apollo's golden head.

Despise a watery hue
And tints that soon expire.
        With fire
Burn thine enamel true.

Twine, twine in artful wise
The blue-green mermaid's arms,
        Mid charms
Of thousand heraldries.

Show in their triple lobe
Virgin and Child, that hold
        Their globe,
Cross-crowned and aureoled.

—All things return to dust
Save beauties fashioned well.
    The bust
Outlasts the citadel.

Oft doth the ploughman's heel,
Breaking an ancient clod,
    Reveal
A Cæsar or a god.

The gods, too, die, alas!
But deathless and more strong
    Than brass
Remains the sovereign song.

Chisel and carve and file,
Till thy vague dream imprint
    Its smile
On the unyielding flint.